MEDIA SOURCES

PHOTOGRAPHY

Published by Creative Education
P.O. Box 227
Mankato, Minnesota 56002
Creative Education is an imprint of The Creative Company.

DESIGN AND PRODUCTION BY **ZENO DESIGN**

PHOTOGRAPHS BY Corbis (Lucien Aigner, Koseph Byron, Henry Diltz),
Getty Images (Pete Atkinson, Martin Barruad, Michael Blann, Mario
Fontes, Gulfimages, Hulton Collection, Hulton Archive/Stringer, Chris
Jackson/Staff, Sarah-Jane Joel, Paul Suterland, Travelpix LTD, William
Henry Fox Talbot/Stringer, Michael Turek, SAM YEH/AFP)

LIBRARY OF CONGRESS CATALOGING-IN-PUBLICATION DATA

Bodden, Valerie.
Photography / by Valerie Bodden.
p. cm. — (Media sources)
Includes index.
ISBN 978-1-58341-558-0
1. Photography—Juvenile literature. 2. Cameras—Juvenile literature.
I. Title. II. Series.

TR149.B485 2008
770—dc22   2006101003

First edition

9 8 7 6 5 4 3 2 1

MEDIA SOURCES

Photography

VALERIE BODDEN

CREATIVE ⬤ EDUCATION

Photographs (*FO-tuh-grafs*) are pictures made by a camera. They are called "photos" for short. Taking photos is called photography (*fo-TAH-graf-ee*).

CAMERAS CAN TAKE PHOTOS OF NATURE

Some people take photos as part of their job. Some people take them for fun. Lots of people like to look at photos!

SOME COMPANIES MAKE CAMERAS FOR KIDS. SOME OF THEM HAVE CARTOON CHARACTERS ON THEM!

SOME PEOPLE GET PAID TO TAKE PHOTOS

The first camera was **invented** about 180 years ago. Before that, there was no way to take photos. Early cameras were big. But the photos they took were small. They were the size of a library card. The photos were not on paper. They were on metal. This made them heavy.

CAMERAS USED TO BE BIG AND HEAVY

At first, it took a long time to take a photo. People had to hold still while they had their photo taken. Sometimes, they had to hold still for as long as 25 minutes!

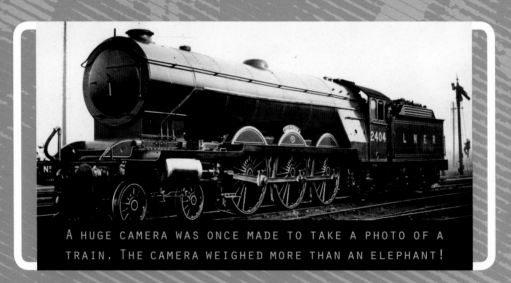

A HUGE CAMERA WAS ONCE MADE TO TAKE A PHOTO OF A TRAIN. THE CAMERA WEIGHED MORE THAN AN ELEPHANT!

THESE WOMEN ARE SITTING FOR A PHOTO

About 120 years ago, a man named George Eastman made **film**. People could put film in a camera. Then they could take lots of photos at a time. When the film was used up, it was made into photos. The photos were printed on special paper.

SOME SPIES USE TINY CAMERAS THAT LOOK LIKE MATCHBOXES OR BUTTONS!

CAMERA FILM IS MADE IN LONG ROLLS

Eastman started a company called Kodak. Kodak made cameras that were small. They were easy to use. All you had to do was press a button. The cameras did not cost much. Some cost only $1! This meant that a lot of people could buy them.

THE FIRST PHOTOS WERE BLACK-AND-WHITE. COLOR PHOTOS HAVE BEEN AROUND ONLY FOR ABOUT 100 YEARS.

KODAK CAMERAS WERE MADE IN FACTORIES

Today, there are all kinds of cameras. Some can take photos of our bones. Others can take photos of the bottom of the ocean. Some can even take photos of outer space!

DISPOSABLE (*DIH-SPO-ZUH-BULL*) CAMERAS TAKE ONE ROLL OF FILM. THEN THEY ARE THROWN AWAY!

SOME CAMERAS CAN GO DEEP UNDERWATER

One new kind of camera is called a digital (*DIJ-ih-tull*) camera. Digital cameras do not use film. They take photos that can be put on a computer.

PEOPLE CAN USE COMPUTERS TO CHANGE PHOTOS FROM A DIGITAL CAMERA. PARTS OF THE PHOTOS CAN EVEN BE ERASED!

MANY PEOPLE USE SMALL DIGITAL CAMERAS

[20]

Today, photos are used for lots of things. They show us new places. They teach us about the past. And they remind us of the fun times in our lives!

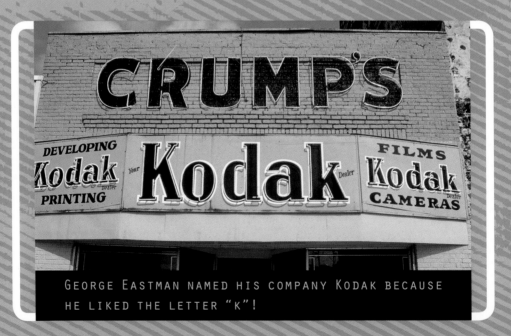

GEORGE EASTMAN NAMED HIS COMPANY KODAK BECAUSE HE LIKED THE LETTER "K"!

[21]

LOTS OF PEOPLE ON VACATION TAKE PHOTOS

GLOSSARY

disposable something that is made to be thrown away after it is used

film a plastic strip that is rolled up and put in cameras to capture photos

invented made for the first time

spies people who try to find out secrets about another person or a country

INDEX